VIRAL VELOCITY

GLOBAL WEB SUCCESS SECRETS

by
Howie Todoit

Dear Esteemed Reader,

Thank you immensely for choosing this book to join your collection. We imagine that you've already embarked on an exploration of ideas within these pages, and we couldn't be happier about it!

Now, if you find yourself chuckling, pondering, or even debating with the words in front of you, we'd absolutely love to hear about it. If you can spare a few moments to pen down your thoughts in a review, we would be as delighted as a dictionary on a spelling bee!

An Amazon review would be excellent - but hey, we're far from picky. Whether it's a scribble on the back of a grocery list, a tweet, or even a message in a bottle (though that might take a while to reach us), your feedback is gold.

Writing a review might not be as fun as a spontaneous dance-off, but we promise it'll bring grins to our faces, warmth to our hearts, and incredibly valuable insights to future readers.

With Gratitude,

Bo Bennett, PhD Publisher Archieboy Holdings, LLC.

TABLE OF CONTENTS

INTRODUCTION

In an ever-evolving digital landscape, an online presence is paramount to success. And not just any online presence; we're talking about a platform that gets shared, re-shared, clicked-on, and chatters about—an entity that goes viral. You see, one of the most compelling advantages of the internet is its potential to spread information, quickly reaching thousands, if not millions, of people. This introduction explores the power and potential of viral content, offering a strong foundation for understanding the principles that will be discussed in detail throughout this book.

"Viral," contrary to its more biological denotation, has been redefined in the internet era. It signifies the exponential growth of web content—articles, videos, images, or any other forms—leading to a massive influx of traffic and visibility. Creating a viral website can turn your business around. It can increase brand recognition, boost exposure, and massively facilitate audience growth—all crucial elements for business success in our digital age.

Going viral, however, isn't solely about spreading content or gaining notoriety. It's also about igniting the world with the uniqueness, innovation, and sheer brilliance of your ideas. When content spreads fast and wide, the chance to impact lives, generate cultural dialogue, inspire action, and ultimately change the world is at your fingertips. That's the real power of having a viral website, with influence echoing beyond the digital hemisphere to the physical world.

But achieving such a phenomenon is easier said than done. It isn't something to stumble upon or just get lucky with. There's a science to it—a blend of strategic planning, understanding of audience behavior, and mastery of the nuanced art of virality. Yes, there's a certain unpredictability to it, but you'll find that the magic of virality often lies in a careful orchestration of various elements.

Whether you are a business owner looking to take your enterprise to the next level, or a newcomer eager to make your market debut, this introduction gives you a sneak peek into the secrets of developing a website that has the potential to go viral. We'll draw from real-life examples and case studies, giving you a comprehensive understanding of how virality has been, and can be, achieved.

Succeeding in the digital space means understanding how to nurture organic growth. Getting away from traditional marketing tactics and delving into the world of organic growth allows a cost-effective and highly efficient way to spread your presence. You'll get the lowdown on organic vs. paid growth, helping you to choose the most beneficial path for your venture.

Of course, anyone with a computer can publish content online, but to resonate globally requires a more nuanced approach. This introduction also serves as an entryway to understanding critical aspects like language and localization, cultural differences, as well as legal and ethical considerations. All these elements are essential to successfully diversify your audience and build a global brand.

Furthermore, creating a global website encompasses more than language and cultural adaptations—it's also tied to global SEO tactics. This book will guide you on how to navigate the world of SEO, helping you to harness the power of search engine algorithms to make your content more accessible and attractive to international audiences.

Social media—the global viral engine—is another instrumental platform that you need to leverage. From Facebook to TikTok, different social media networks have unique strengths. We need to understand these dynamics in order to harness their power. We'll tackle proven strategies and delve into emerging platforms to guide you on how to construct content that encourages shares, likes, and interaction.

If the digital world is your ocean, data analytics is your compass. Web analytics bear the keys to understanding your audience, your content, and the impact of your strategies. We'll share with you the basics of web analytics, how to measure virality, and ultimately, how to make data-driven decisions that can propel your website to viral status.

Lastly, we recognize that sometimes, the best way to learn is by example. So, we'll guide you through a diverse range of case studies showcasing successful global websites. This will inspire you, and provide practical, tangible examples of the principles and strategies we'll cover.

This is not just a book—it's a comprehensive guide to making websites go viral. Consider it a journey, during which you'll be armed with the strategies, intelligence, and insights needed to turn your website from a static existence into a dynamic, viral phenomenon.

Think of the audience as your guide, the content as your vehicle, and data analytics as your roadmap. Together, they'll equip you to traverse this exhilarating journey. It's an adventure that is as powerful as it is illuminating, and we're here to make sure you're prepared for every leap, turn, and obstacle on your path to creating a viral website. So, let's get started, shall we?

CHAPTER 1

The Power of Going Viral

As we forge ahead from the introductory ideas dished out in the last section, it's time to delve into the heart of the matter - the exceptional force that is 'going viral'. Remember when Pokémon Go had a grip on an entire generation or when everyone was pouring buckets of iced water over their heads and filming it? That, my friend, is the power of virality. Now, substitute that scenario with your website garnering similar attention - unimaginable, right? Guess what, it's entirely feasible! The concept of 'viral' is the epitome of exponential growth and taps into the core of our interconnected social structures. When your website content hits the nerve of shared human experiences, emotions, or values, it rides the wave of mass sharing, snowballing into the realm of 'viral'. The delighted surprise of a hilarious meme, the shared outrage sparked by a news story, or even the communal camaraderie of entertaining contests - they all have the potential to turn your website into the next web sensation. Yet, it's essential to remember that virality doesn't just occur by chance, it's a consciously nurtured process, backed by an understanding of your audience, mastery of your content, and strategic use of social media channels. Let's cut to the chase and unravel this fascinating world of virality.

DEFINING VIRALITY

The term 'virality' has become a buzzword in the digital age, often associated with websites, online content, and digital marketing

4

strategies that have achieved an exceptional level of shares, views, or interactions on the internet.

But what exactly is 'virality'? In its most fundamental definition, virality is the phenomenon of a piece of content spreading rapidly on the internet through social media and word-of-mouth. It's like a virus that spreads from one host to another, infecting more people until it eventually becomes widespread or 'goes viral'.

It's important to understand, though, that virality goes beyond just a large number of views. It represents a momentum of shareability that can cause a sudden surge in popularity. When a website or a piece of content goes viral, it exponentially multiplies its reach as people share it with their networks.

Although this sounds like a dream come true for any website owner or entrepreneur, making your website go viral isn't as straightforward as it might seem. Virality isn't simply a numbers game. It hinges on the perfect balance of various elements such as audience interest, timing, platform, and most importantly, the content itself.

This brings us to the 'content' part of virality - a crucial aspect. Viral content typically has unique characteristics that excite, amuse, surprise, or connect with audiences on an emotional level. Whether it's a fascinating blog post, a shocking news story, or a gripping video, the hook is usually something that incites immediate reaction and motivates sharing.

Everything on the internet can be shared, but only a fraction of it actually goes viral. Virality comes into play when a website or piece of content not only reaches its intended audience but also convinces them to become ambassadors, actively sharing it with their own networks. This cascading word-of-mouth effect fuels the viral spread.

Though at times viral success may seem serendipitous, there's an underlying science to it. Virality can be stimulated by understanding your audience's psychology, aligning your content with their interests, and delivering it in a compelling, shareable format. It's not just about sparking interest, but sustaining it long enough for it to spread like wildfire.

It's also worth pointing out that virality isn't a feat achievable by every kind of website or content. Some content, by their very nature, have a higher propensity to go viral than others. Informative, entertaining, emotionally resonant content often creates a fertile ground for virality as compared to dry, uninspiring content.

The platform on which the content is shared also significantly influences its potential for virality. Social media platforms, with their massive active user base and easy sharing mechanisms, serve as the optimal launchpads for viral content. However, unsuccessful attempts at virality are far more common than successful ones.

Here's the reality - not every website will go viral. It's a grueling endeavor that requires delving into the depths of user psychology, testing different strategies, and continuously optimizing content for the ever-changing algorithmic landscape of the internet.

That being said, virality presents an immense opportunity for businesses. A part of your website or a particular piece of content going viral can boost brand recognition, increase website traffic, and even boost sales dramatically. Just remember, virality shouldn't be the only metric for success; it's equally important to focus on creating consistent, quality content that resonates with your audience over time.

Keep in mind that the virality of a website or content is not permanent. It is fleeting, much like how a virus spreads and then disappears. Therefore, while virality can provide a quick boost, sustainable growth requires persistent effort and strategic planning.

Ultimately, understanding virality is key to leveraging its power effectively. It's about taking that leap, spreading your unique brand story, and hopefully, watching it unfold into a viral phenomenon. In the following chapters, we will delve into the nuances of what makes content shareable, audience behavior, and strategies to nurture organic growth, providing you with a roadmap to viral success.

CASE STUDIES OF VIRAL WEBSITES

Every entrepreneur and website owner dreams of creating the next big viral site, but virality isn't just a game of chance. It comes from a combination of fresh idea, engaging content and smart strategy. Let's explore some real-world examples of phenomenal viral successes to learn what went right in each case.

The Huffington Post: Launched in 2005, The Huffington Post rapidly gained popularity through its unique approach to presenting news and information. It used web 2.0 technology, a blend of news aggregation, blogs, and original content. The launch timing was perfect; social media use was on the rise, providing a platform for the content to go viral. Fresh, frequently updated content drew in users, and the comment section beneath each article helped create an engaged community.

BuzzFeed: BuzzFeed is another classic example of viral content done right. Starting as a side project, BuzzFeed incorporated quizzes, listicles, and intentionally sharable content, setting the stage for an explosion in user engagement. The elements of fun, surprise, and nostalgia in BuzzFeed posts led to mass shares on social media platforms.

Upworthy: Upworthy successfully turned going viral into an art form. The site specializes in feel-good, positive news and stories that people are likely to share with an uplifting tagline. Combining a unique storyboard style of storytelling with emotionally charged content and a curiosity-inducing headline, Upworthy went viral within months of its launch.

ViralNova: Launched in 2013, this one-man blog quickly reached tens of millions of monthly visitors. Using emotionally-charged, sensational headlines compelled readers to click, read, and share content. Despite being called "clickbait," the strategy earned ViralNova a spot among the top 200 sites in the U.S, proving that intriguing headlines truly resonate with an audience.

Unilad and LadBible: Targeting the 18 to 34-year-old demographic, these British sites used humor, memes, and trending content to engage users. Understanding their defined audience has allowed these platforms to flourish, proving that knowing your target demographic is crucial to going viral.

The Ice Bucket Challenge: Although not a website, it's worth mentioning the Ice Bucket Challenge, a viral phenomenon like no other. Promoted by the ALS Association, this campaign involved dumping a bucket of ice water on someone's head and recording it. The initiative not only raised awareness about ALS but also brought in $115 million in donations. It was the gripping visual content, personal engagement, and dedicated purpose that underpinned its sensational spread.

Dollar Shave Club: While not a content-based website, Dollar Shave Club astoundingly disrupted the razor industry with a simple, humorous, and highly shareable video. The company's launch video went viral within days, underscoring the power of shareable videos.

The Oatmeal: The Oatmeal's success lies in its humorous and eccentric comics that represent relatable life events and concepts. The high shareability and wide appeal of this content have contributed to its remarkable virality.

ZergNet: This site hosts links to interesting articles on other websites. The key to ZergNet's success lies in partnering with publishers for content exchange, ensuring a constant stream of engaging articles for visitors, driving millions of visits per month.

Flappy Bird: This mobile game quickly went viral due to its simplicity and frustrating difficulty, proving that sometimes, less is more when it comes to feeding into the public's appetite for viral content.

Each of these case studies offers a unique insight into the factors that contribute to a website going viral. Whether it's a clear understanding of the target audience, engaging content that people want to share, or a unique value proposition, there are many pathways to virality. The key is to study successful examples and adapt them to your business model and audience.

Going viral is about hooking into your audience's emotions, curiosity, and desires. From creating engaging content that resonates with your audience, to developing compelling calls to action, and leveraging social networks, there's much to learn from these viral website case studies.

Remember, each of these sites tapped into a particular zeitgeist at their time of launch. The content they produced appealed to emotions, be it laughter, shock, curiosity, or compassion, causing people to share it. Likewise, aim to understand your audience and what influences their behavior, then create content that taps into these insights.

So, it's time to get imaginative and start building your road to viral success. With observed strategies from these case studies, a dash of ingenuity, and plentiful data-driven decisions, you're well on your way to making your website a viral sensation.

CHAPTER 2

The Science of Virality

As we delve further into the fascinating realm of virality, it's critical to understand that it's not just about a stroke of luck or some inexplicable, magical marketing mojo. Instead, it's deeply rooted in science, where specific elements can tremendously increase the chances of content going viral. But what makes content shareable? At the crux of it, shareable content typically provides value, captivates emotions, caters to the audience's interests, and is primed for easy sharing. To create such content, you need to truly understand your audience's behavior. Are they motivated by humor or do they lean more towards emotional, inspiring stories? Do they prefer bite-sized content they can consume on-the-go or long-form pieces? Crack the code of your audience's behavior, and you'll have a powerful lever for virality at your disposal. However, remember that while understanding the science of virality can guide your strategy, at the heart of every viral phenomenon lies unique, engaging content that resonates with the audience.

WHAT MAKES CONTENT SHAREABLE?

Before we discuss what makes content shareable, it's important to understand that content creation is more than just putting words on digital paper. It's an art that merges creativity, strategy, and a deep understanding of the intended audience. So, what are the elements that make content so intriguing that readers can't help but share it?

Firstly, let's consider the essential role that emotions play. Content that triggers an emotional response tends to be more shareable. If your content can evoke happiness, surprise, anger, or even sadness, it's likely to be shared more and hence gain greater virality. It's crucial to understand your audience's preferences and craft your content to hit those emotional checks. After all, people share content if it gives them a certain feeling, be it a sense of belonging or merely a hearty laugh.

Secondly, let's shed light on the power of relevancy. Content that is timely, contextual, and relevant to your audience is more likely to be shared. If you're writing about a trending topic or a recent event, you're more likely to catch the attention of your readers. Your audience will feel more driven to share this content because it is their way of staying current and contributing to the ongoing conversations within their networks.

Thirdly, usability and accessibility are crucial factors in making content shareable. Regardless of how compelling and relevant your content may be, if it's challenging to share, then it simply won't be. People should be allowed to share your content effortlessly, by incorporating direct share buttons for different social media platforms. Equally important is making sure that your content is easily digestible with simple words, clear sentences, and engaging visuals.

Moreover, high-quality content is more likely to be passed around. When we say 'high-quality,' we don't just mean well-written; we mean that it provides value to the reader. Consider focusing on delivering unique insights, well-researched facts, or practical advice. The goal is to provide value so that the reader learns something new or gains a fresh perspective. This triggers them to share this newfound knowledge with others.

Another critical factor is the story woven into the content. Stories allow readers to connect with your content on a deeper level, making it more memorable and more likely to be shared. Whether it's a case study, a personal anecdote, or a client success story, this narrative form caters to the human fascination with stories, stirring emotions and generating a more significant impact.

Creating content that resonates with your audience's values and beliefs can also boost its shareability. Building content that aligns with your readers' identities can enhance the credibility of your brand and increase reader loyalty. People are generally more willing to share content that represents them and communicates who they are to others.

Adding a dose of humor where it fits could also make your content more shareable. Who doesn't like to laugh or bring a smile to someone's face? Humor can add an enjoyable and memorable twist to your content, making it irresistible to share.

Visual elements in your content can drastically increase its shareability. In a realm where time is often limited, images, infographics, or videos can provide quick insights and make content more engaging. They also encourage sharing by adding color, breaking up text, and providing variety for the reader.

Interactive content often gets shared and engages your audience in a way static content can't. This can come in various forms, like quizzes, polls, or interactive infographics. Interactive content not only is amusing but provides a personal element to content consumption as it allows audiences to participate directly.

Let's not forget the influence of social proof on content shareability. Testimonials, reviews, or any form of user-generated content add authenticity and credibility to your content, encouraging more shares. Viewers tend to trust and share content that others have approved or enjoyed.

In essence, creating shareable content is about considering these factors and integrating them into your content strategy. A balance is key; a useful piece of content may not necessarily invoke strong emotions or have a story to tell. Different content will have different strengths, but understanding these attributes helps in aiming for that sweet spot where your content is not merely informative but immersively engaging and inherently shareable.

Keep in mind that developing shareable content is not about using every single element described here but rather picking and choosing what works best for your audience and your brand. These are tools, and like all tools, they perform best when used wisely.

Ultimately, knowing your audience remains the constant factor in determining shareability. If you understand who you are trying to reach, what resonates with them, and how they consume and share content, you are well on your way to creating content that flies organically across the digital space.

UNDERSTANDING AUDIENCE BEHAVIOR

The magic of virality often springs from a deep understanding of the habits and preferences of your audience. This knowledge is what helps you create content that connects with them and leads them to share it with people in their circles. This turns into a ripple effect sending your brand's message to numerous corners of the internet world in no time at all.

Getting into the heads of your audience implies understanding their motivations, preferences, and behaviors. This comprehension is crucial because sharing varies considerably with different types of audiences. Let's dive deeper into the importance of understanding audience behavior for viral success.

Your audience is likely diverse, each with unique needs and points of view. They're also at different stages in their relationship with your brand. Therefore, the concept of audience segmentation becomes pertinent. It can lead to creating more personalized content, which resonates better with each segment and increases the likelihood of sharing.

Audience segmentation isn't solely dependent on demographics; it's recommended to also look at psychographics. These include information about your audience's interests, pain points, values, and attitudes. This provides a more nuanced, comprehensive picture of your audience, leading to the creation of content that is shareable.

Knowing when your audience is most active can also impact the virality of the content. This information can be discovered through analytics and enables you to post the content when it is most likely to be seen, interacted with, and shared. Correspondingly, understanding what type of content your audience prefers can also boost your chances of your content going viral.

Some audiences might prefer long-form articles, others might be more inclined to click on an infographic, while some might be into quick video clips or love scrolling through visually appealing images. Understanding their preference will empower you to create content that your audience can't resist sharing. Hence, different audiences have different content consumption habits, and knowing these habits can be game-changing.

The platform your audience prefers also matters in the context of virality. Different platforms attract different demographics - Facebook attracts a different set than Snapchat, for instance. If you understand your audience's preferred platform, you can tailor your content format to what is best suited for that platform, thereby increasing the likelihood of shares.

Carrying out surveys and polls can also equip you with audience insights. You can ask your audience directly about the type of content they'd like to see more of, the issues they're facing, or what they think about your products or services. This type of feedback can lead to you creating improved content with higher potential for sharing.

One classic error in understand audience behavior is assuming it's static. It's crucial to understand that audience behavior is dynamic and consistently changing due to numerous factors including changes in technology trends, cultural shifts, and personal circumstances. Therefore, continuously monitoring, adjusting, and realigning your strategy based on the evolving behavior of your audience is pivotal.

Social listening is an effective method for understanding this evolving behavior. By tracking and analyzing online conversations about your brand, competitors, or industry, you can gain insights into your audience's attitudes, interests, and concerns that they might not openly share. These insights can reveal the type of content your audience is most likely to engage with and share, improving your chances of going viral.

Lastly, it's important not to underestimate the power of emotion in understanding audience behavior. Emotional engagement can often be the trigger that leads to sharing. If your content is amusing, shocking, heartwarming, or inspiring, it is more likely to be shared. In this light, understanding what kind of emotions resonate most with your audience is important for virality.

As you can see, a deep understanding of audience behavior is crucial to virality. It helps you create content that resonates with your audience, inspires them to share it, and ultimately boosts your chances of your website going viral. When your audience feels connected to your content, they will want their network to feel the same way. This is the essence of the ripple effect that leads to virality.

Remember, virality isn't accidental. It's a skill that can be mastered. A deep understanding of your audience's behavior is one crucial element of this skill. Equipped with this knowledge, you are on your way to making your website go viral.

CHAPTER 3

Nurturing Organic Growth

As our dive into the science of virality culminated, it's time to shift our focus towards nurturing organic growth. Organic growth, often the backbone of a viral website's success, emphasizes the crucial role of authentic engagement and development. Yet achieving it isn't a cakewalk—it requires a keen understanding of your audience and the deployment of strategic measures that encourage natural progression. For website owners, striking a balance between organic growth and paid growth can feel like a tightrope walk. On one hand, you have the allure of immediate results from paid growth strategies, but the authenticity and scalability of organic growth remain unbeatable. This chapter intends to stress how these organic growth strategies, when executed right, can provide you with a solid foundation that not only boosts your website's ranking but also establishes its viral potential. From fostering user generated content, ensuring regular updates, to engaging and educating your user base organically—each effort adds up to bolster your website's chances at virality. So, let's set the stage for a journey towards sustained, natural, and progressive growth.

THE IMPORTANCE OF ORGANIC GROWTH

After understanding the science of virality and the elements that make content shareable, let's delve into an equally important aspect of growing your website: organic growth. But, first, why is organic growth crucial? Why should website owners and entrepreneurs focus on this kind of growth?

Organic growth is the natural progression that comes from the core activities of your business. It's about acquiring new customers, driving more traffic, increasing user interactions, and fostering genuine relationships with your audience. Organic growth is built, not bought. It's slower but steadier. It doesn't rely on fickle algorithms or costly ad campaigns.

In the web world, organic growth means gaining followers, generating traffic, and increasing conversions without relying heavily on paid advertising. This involves creating high-quality content, improving SEO, and actively engaging with your audience. These methods tend to attract a more loyal and engaged audience than paid strategies.

The magic of organic growth lies in its authenticity. When your website growth is organic, it means that people are genuinely interested in what you offer. They like your content, appreciate your brand voice, and trust your authenticity. This kind of connection with your audience is more likely to create loyal customers who'll come back to your website again and again.

The beauty of organic growth is that it tends to compound over time. Sure, it might approach the race like a tortoise rather than a hare, but remember - the tortoise wins in the end. This growth can lead to a robust, large, and dedicated audience base you can rely on.

Another bonus point for organic growth is that it is cost-effective. You are not paying for ads to get your content or your website seen. Instead, you rely on your excellent content and positive user experiences. While this may require significant time and effort at the start, the ROI can be well worth it as organic growth is usually more sustainable in the long run.

Furthermore, websites that grow organically enjoy better search engine rankings. Search engines prioritize sites that deliver quality content and provide an excellent user experience. Therefore, if you continuously work on your organic growth by enhancing your content and user interactions, you are also boosting your SEO rankings. This, in turn, only serves to further fuel your organic growth - it's a virtuous cycle.

Organic growth also provides valuable insights into your audience. It helps understand what your audience likes, shares, and how they interact with your website. These insights can guide further strategies, content creation, and more.

In essence, the importance of organic growth lies in its ability to create a steady stream of traffic, loyal customers, and lasting brand lovers. It contributes significantly to the trustworthiness and credibility of your business, which are key principles for any business looking to make a lasting impact.

That being said, it's essential to remember that organic growth doesn't happen overnight. It's a process that requires patience, persistence, and a pinch of creativity. It's about creating a solid foundation for your website, fostering trust and loyalty among your audience, and continuously refining and improving your strategies based on changing trends and audience behaviors.

Do not get discouraged if things seem slow at first. Organic growth is about building deep roots for your website, creating a solid footing that will allow you to weather changes in online trends and consumer behaviors. The resilience you build during this phase will be your armor against swift and short-lived viral hypes.

Finally, remember that the road to growth, while seemingly endless, is a journey, not a destination. It's about progress, not perfection. By focusing on organic growth, you're nourishing your website to grow stronger and healthier, enabling it to bear fruit even in the toughest of seasons.

In the next section, we'll delve deeper into specific strategies to foster organic growth. These strategies will be the fertile soil wherein you can sow and cultivate the seeds of your website's growth. The journey to virality begins with a single step, and that step is fostering organic growth.

STRATEGIES FOR ORGANIC GROWTH

What you've been waiting for! Strategies for organic growth. When we talk about organic growth, we're considering the natural, unforced evolution of your website's popularity over time, free from jumps and jolts. Sounds like the dream, right? Let's get to it.

First off, **content is king**. It's your site's lifeblood and the primary reason people will ever come calling. Can't stress this enough, create high-quality content that's valuable and relevant to your target audience. Think about what problems they may have, and how your content can act as the solution. By offering solutions, you become a credible and trusted source of information in your industry.

Crucial to this, of course, is understanding your audience. What do they want? What do they need? Use analytics to your advantage here. Knowing who your audience is, and where they come from, will help you cater more directly to their interests, and bring an added touch of personalization to your content.

Beyond quality content, consider your **website's design**. Is your site easy to navigate? Is it accessible and user-friendly? A good user experience will earn your site more return visits. Prioritize your website's performance, including page load speeds. Slow load times can not only discourage visitors but also impact your site's SEO.

That takes us to our next point, **SEO**. To drive organic growth, it is essential to ensure your website is optimized for search engines. Use relevant keywords and meta descriptions, prioritize on-page SEO, and invest time and effort in building high-quality backlinks. Making it easier for search engines to find your site increases the visibility and, thus, draws in more organic traffic.

Another game-changing strategy is **blogging**. This time-tested tactic continues to be a significant driver of success. Blogs provide a platform to share fresh and high-quality content frequently, which not only provided increased value for readers but can also improve your ranking in search engine results.

Never underestimate the power of **social media**! Social media channels can act as an amplifier for your content, increasing its reach and boosting your organic growth. Share your content on all applicable social networks to increase exposure and drive traffic back to your site.

Here comes an often overlooked strategy; **forming strategic partnerships**. A right partner can not only increase your website's exposure but also presents cross-promotion opportunities. It's all about finding a complementary business or entity and determining how you can mutually benefit one another. Remember, it's a two-way street!

This next one might sound formal, but has practical benefits - **public speaking**. Presenting at conferences, workshops, and webinars can help position you as an expert in your field and increase your website's exposure. Consider it an opportunity for some well-earned limelight!

Also, don't forget **email marketing**. It is an effective, highly cost-effective strategy that, when done right, can significantly increase your site's organic growth. Building and maintaining a mailing list keeps your audience engaged and informed about new content or offerings on your website.

You should also consider the immense value of **guest posting**. By contributing to other similar, high-quality blogs or sites, you can reach a broader audience, earn backlinks, and establish authority in your industry. Remember, pick your hosts wisely!

Lastly, but certainly not least, is the **personal touch**. Engaging directly with your audience whether it's through responding to comments, social media engagement, or customer support, forms a relationship that encourages repeated visits. Customer engagement results in loyal followers, which is the surest way to steady organic growth.

Well, that's a list of some proven strategies for organic growth. They all need consistency and patience, but remember - the best things come to those who wait! Your website's popularity isn't a race, but a marathon, and organic growth is the surest path to long-lasting success.

ORGANIC GROWTH VS. PAID GROWTH

Let's not lose sight of our previous discussions on the importance of organic growth and strategies for fostering it. More so, let's turn our attention to a comparison that often emerges: organic growth versus paid growth. Is one superior to the other? Does it make sense to focus solely on one while disregarding the other? Understanding the distinctions and the relationship between these two growth strategies is paramount for website owners and entrepreneurs aiming to make their websites go viral.

Organic growth, as we've noted before, is a natural momentum driven by the value users perceive from your site or content. It occurs when people voluntarily share your content, recommend your website or speak highly of it because they genuinely appreciate what you're offering. It can be slow initially, but its power often lies in its ability to create a long-term, loyal audience base.

On the other hand, paid growth revolves around investing capital into marketing strategies such as advertising and pay-per-click campaigns. Paid growth can boost your site's visibility quickly and help draw in a substantial number of new visitors. It's a more immediate, but often less sustainable way, of driving traffic to your site.

The crucial thing about organic growth is that it's much more than a flavor-of-the-month strategy; it's a mentality that focuses on providing valuable content that resonates with your audience. It's about understanding your users, what they want, and providing it consistently. This helps in building trust and loyalty, hence fostering a community of devoted fans who can't help but spread the word about your site.

Paid growth, however, has its charm too. It offers a quick increase in traffic and presents an opportunity to target specific segments of potential audiences. It may be particularly beneficial when you're launching a new site or when you've fine-tuned your offering and want to attract new visitors quickly and in large numbers.

There's a misconception that paid growth is tantamount to cheating or taking the easy way out. Not so. Yes, it involves spending money but that doesn't devalue the process. When you invest capital in paid growth strategies, you're essentially paying to reach potential customers faster. However, converting these users into loyal visitors or customers is still up to the relevancy and quality of your content.

A significant downside of paid growth is that, once you stop the paid campaigns, the traffic may dwindle, highlighting its potentially fleeting nature. In contrast, organic growth tends to be more sustainable and lasting, as its built on the foundation of the inherently shareable and valuable content, along with a loyal audience coming back for more.

It begs the question, should you go for organic or paid growth?

The answer isn't binary; it's rarely a question of choosing one over the other but more about harmonizing the two. Using both strategies in tandem can optimize your site's growth. The key is to strike a balance that caters to your brand's unique needs and objectives.

For instance, you might use paid growth strategies to give your brand an initial boost, creating visibility and drawing in users. From there, your focus can shift to delivering high-quality content consistently, engaging with your audience, and other organic growth strategies which would keep those users coming back and spreading the word about you.

An integrated growth strategy affords you the benefits of both worlds: the quick results of paid campaigns and the long-term sustainability of organic growth. This complementary approach often proves more successful than relying on one strategy alone.

The process won't always be straightforward. It requires a continuous cycle of monitoring, analyzing, learning, and adjusting. However, taking the time to understand these growth strategies will provide a broader perspective on how to approach the growth of your website.

So, as website owners and entrepreneurs working to make their sites go viral, don't pit organic growth against paid growth. Instead, view both as different gears in your viral engine, each playing its role in propelling your site's virality. Understand their differences, balance their use, and let them collectively propel your website to newfound heights.

Keep in mind also that the viral journey is more a marathon than a sprint. Aim not just for an immediate explosion in traffic, but a steady, long-term increase built on the consistency of valuable content and unwavering user trust.

CHAPTER 4

Building a Global Website

Following the focus on organic growth, it's time we delve into the specifics of constructing a website that embraces global reach. To facilitate a worldwide impact, it's not enough just to translate your content. True global appeal needs a concordance of language localization and a perceptive understanding of cultural intricacies. Not only will your site need to interpret the semantics of various lingual nuances accurately, but it'll also need to depict and respect cultural norms and values inherent to different regions. Think of gestures and expressions that resonate with the locals. For instance, a thumbs-up may signify approval in the U.S., but it could be interpreted as offensive in some Middle Eastern countries. Sensitivity to such intercultural divergences fosters goodwill and trust among your international demographics.

Furthermore, creating a website with international appeal also poses various legal and ethical conundrums such as user privacy laws are changing worldwide, and companies are required to have transparent privacy policies. Complying with these regulations not only keeps your website on the right side of the law but also heightens your credibility among users who are increasingly concerned about how their data is used. We will construe these elements and approach how cohesive integration can be achieved in this chapter, ensuring your website doesn't just reach a global audience, but engages them effectively too.

LANGUAGE AND LOCALIZATION CONSIDERATIONS

As we aspire to build a globally recognized website, we must take into account the importance of language and localization. Having our content accessible to a wide range of audiences involves more than simply translating words. It requires a comprehensive understanding of varying cultures, languages, and individual regions. Effectively localized content could determine whether your site goes viral – or flatlines.

Firstly, think about how your content communicates with non-English speakers. It's no secret that English is a lingual heavyweight on the global stage. That said, large, influential markets speak other languages. Cater to them to amplify your impact. Mandarin Chinese, Spanish, and Arabic speakers - to name a few - constitute a considerable potential user base. Consider having your content translated and localized to meet their needs.

Translating isn't merely converting words from one language to another. It's about capturing the essence, the tone, and the voice of your brand in another language. This means selecting the right phrases, idioms, expressions, and cultural references that are relevant to your target audience. A poorly translated website can give off an unprofessional impression to foreign users and can even lead to misinterpretation of the brand's message.

There's more to it, though. It's not always enough to just translate your content correctly. Localization takes translation a step further and modifies the content to fit the culture, customs, and expectations of the target audience. It's about creating an experience that feels native to your users, regardless of where they are in the world.

For instance, remember that not all countries use the same units of measurement, date format, or currency. Tailoring your website based on these details can make a significant difference in how welcoming your site feels to users from different regions. Localization management software can help with this, ensuring seamless conversion between units applicable to different regions.

A crucial detail to consider under the umbrella of localization is the layout of your website. Languages that read from right to left, like Arabic and Hebrew, will require a different design structure than those that read from left to right. Ignoring this could result in a website that feels awkward and unintuitive to those users.

Moving on to the selection of local languages. Why limit yourself to a single, global version of your website? With the help of internationalized domain names (IDN), you can design URLs in different languages for different regions. This is a surefire way to make your website feel local and inviting globally.

Moreover, recognize your audience's dialect differences when localizing content. For instance, Spanish in Spain is different from Latin American Spanish. The same goes for French from France and Quebecois from Canada. Understanding these nuances can make your website genuinely resonate with the desired market.

Don't skip considering local search engines and social media platforms either. Google might reign indeed globally, but regional search engines like Baidu in China and Yandex in Russia play major roles in their respective countries. Similarly, while Facebook and Twitter are popular worldwide, Staiger in Estonia or Vkontakte in Russia have immense popularity. Catering to these platforms in the relevant countries can boost your site's virality immensely.

Let's not forget the significance of color in localization. Different cultures express different meanings through colors. While white may signify purity or peace in Western cultures, it symbolizes mourning in Eastern ones. Acknowledge this in your website design to avoid sending mixed or offensive messages to your audience.

As you embrace website localization, take time to get quality translators proficient in the native language. Machine translation can lead to errors and mismatched meanings. Worse, algorithms fail to capture the cultural cues and nuances that a human translator can.

Lastly, once you've considered these elements, testing is crucial. Nothing beats direct feedback from your users. You can pilot your localized website in smaller markets first. Gathering feedback can help iron out any unnoticed cultural faux pas or translation errors while encouraging essential granular insights.

In conclusion, understand and adapt to various global languages, cultures, customs, and considerations. This will help take your website to the next level in the global scene. Language and localization might just be the final cog in the machine that is your viral website.

LEGAL AND ETHICAL CONSIDERATIONS

When it comes to building a global website with the aim of going viral, there's a lot more to consider than just getting your content noticed. Legal and ethical issues can often stand as unanticipated stumbling blocks, potentially pulling your website down if not adequately addressed. These factors are as crucial as the flashy design or killer content you look forward to showcasing.

First things first: Understand that internet law varies widely from one country to the other. What's legal and commonplace in one region can be restricted and penalized in another. It's important to get insights into the laws and regulations about internet usage in the countries or regions you're targeting.

Let's begin with copyright laws. They ensure intellectual property rights are respected globally. When uploading any content, be it text, images, or music, ensure it's legally yours to use. Ignoring copyrights could lead to legal disputes and soil your brand's reputation.

Relatedly, let's talk about trademarks. Names, logos, and slogans that brand your business should be checked for potential legal infringement. It ensures your branding doesn't collide with an already existing brand. As you'll discover, a legal wrangle over trademarks is the last thing a budding website needs.

Also, when determining the legality of your website's content, you ought to consider Advertisements law. This aspect becomes significant if you are planning on including commercials or endorsements. Accurate disclosure, transparency, and adherence to the relevant ad laws of the targeted regions are non-negotiables.

Now, let's move on to privacy policies. A transparent privacy policy that outlines how you collect, store, and use visitor information is a must. With the recent implementation of GDPR (General Data Protection Regulation) in the EU and similar regulations elsewhere, maintaining user privacy and data protection is more critical than ever.

Data localization laws are another area to pay attention to. Some countries require that data associated with their citizens be stored within their borders. If you're serving customers in such regions, you may need to invest in local data centers or cloud services that comply.

User-generated content is something else you need to be wary about. If your website allows visitors to upload their own content, you need to make sure that this doesn't infringe someone else's rights. For this, implementing a clear policy and mechanism to handle such instances will go a long way.

No discussion of legal considerations for a global website would be complete without addressing the law of defamation. Avoid posting content that can adversely affect someone's reputation. The potential for legal action makes this a critical factor to consider.

If your website is designed to target children, there are particular sets of regulations, like COPPA (Children's Online Privacy Protection Act) in the US, which needs to be adhered to closely. Such laws often restrict the collection of information and enforce strict parental controls.

On top of legal considerations, ethical considerations are just as cardinal. Ethical considerations extend beyond legal requirements and into realms of content appropriateness, respect for cultural variances, fairness in serving all user groups, responsible marketing, etc. Maintaining a solid set of ethics forms the solid backbone of your brand and often decides how your audiences perceive you.

High on the ethical considerations list are cultural sensitivity and respect for diversity. What's conceived as normal in one culture might be offensive in another. Making your website culturally adaptable and non-offensive to your global audience is crucial in establishing a successful global footprint.

Moving on, digital accessibility is another important ethical consideration. By making your website accessible to all visitors, including those with disabilities, you're not only abiding by legal standards such as the ADA (Americans with Disabilities Act) but also demonstrating a strong commitment to ethical inclusivity.

Lastly, remember that while you're trying to rush to ensure your website goes viral, don't forget to build trust and credibility. Maintain absolute honesty and clarity in all your global customer dealings and remember, your online reputation is built on how well you navigate these legal and ethical considerations. Remember, a robust ethical reputation tends to travel faster in virtual space than even the finest viral content.

CHAPTER 5

International SEO Tactics

With your global website now up and running, it's time to delve into the fascinating world of International SEO tactics that can significantly enhance your site's visibility across multiple geographical locations. Finesse in keyword research plays a pivotal role in this endeavour. You need to identify those potent search terms that resonate with the global audience and fit seamlessly into your website's content. Tools like Google Keyword Planner and SEMrush can lend a helping hand in this exploration. However, universal appeal isn't enough; your SEO strategy must embrace local linguistic nuances for optimizing search results, hence the importance of Geo-Targeting. By setting your geographic preference in Google Search Console and incorporating location-specific keywords in your SEO, you're telling the search engine exactly where your target audience is. This tailored approach, whilst maintaining a global appeal, ensures your content reaches those who'll find it most engaging, aiding your pursuit of virality. So, don't keep waiting! It's time to go global with your SEO tactics, maximising the reach and impact of your viral content.

GLOBAL KEYWORD RESEARCH

Let's sweep away any misconception you might have that keyword research is a uniform task, identical for every place on the globe. As attractive as that sounds, we are dealing with people from different corners of the world. The words they use, how they use them, and what they search for varies drastically based on their regional background, culture, and consumer habits. Therefore, global keyword research is integral to International SEO.

It's not as simple as taking your top keywords and translating them into the local language. It's a more challenging, yet fulfilling, endeavor. You need to think like your target audience, using their language, spelling, and colloquial terms. The trusty technique we all love and use intuitively is empathy. So, what are the steps in global keyword research? Let's delve deeper.

First things first - Identify your target markets. Look at your website analytics and identify where the majority of your traffic is coming from. Also consider where you want to grow your presence. Once you have this information, you'll know the languages and regions for your keyword research.

Dig into the culturally relevant key terms your potential customers might be using. This requires an intricate understanding of the local language and culture. It's good to hire native speakers and cultural experts for this purpose. Several keyword tools can help you with this, but remember, there's no replacement for human insight.

Then, build your keyword list. Inclusion is critical here. Don't just stick to popular, high-volume keywords. Remember to include long-tail keywords and phrases used by locals. These terms might not generate tons of traffic, but they often lead to higher conversions.

Now, it is time for search intent. Understanding what people mean when they use certain search terms in your target market is crucial. For instance, in America, when people search for "football," they mean American football, not soccer. Recognizing such nuances can have a significant impact on the relevance and accuracy of your keywords.

Once you have your preliminary list of keywords, analyze their competitiveness. Certain keywords dominate search engine results, and it's vital to know how tough it might be to rank for them. SEO software can generate keyword difficulty scores that provide a clear picture.

The next step is localizing your keywords to ensure that they're in line with the vernacular and search trends of your target markets. Online tools and translators are of help, yes, but don't solely rely on them. Get native speakers to review your localized keyword list.

Your global keyword strategy isn't set in stone—it should be fluid and adapt to changes in language and search habits. Regularly reviewing your global keywords will ensure you're always on top of the ever-changing language landscape.

Remember, SEO isn't just about ranking high on search engines. It's about delivering quality content that answers the searcher's queries. With a well-drawn-out global keyword strategy in place, you're not only answering their queries but also speaking their language - quite literally!

This approach does make the process more time-consuming and complex but also adds that sweet flavor of authenticity to your SEO strategy. A flavor that your target audience can relish, and once they know that you speak their language, they are more likely to trust you. Trust us, when they do, the rewards you reap will be worth it!

Lastly, don't forget to measure the performance of your keywords. Use analytics tools to track how your keywords are performing in different regions. This information will help in making data-driven decisions regarding keyword optimization. Remember, despite your best efforts, not every keyword will be a success, and that's okay. It's all part of the process, and each step taken is a learning experience.

In conclusion, global keyword research is a lot more than picking a series of buzzwords. It leans heavily on the ability to empathize with different cultures and understand their consumption of language. It requires patience, grit, and the willingness to get it wrong first, to get it right eventually. Don't be afraid to make mistakes, they eventually lead to a refined, effective global keyword strategy, positioning you well for international SEO success.

GEO-TARGETING AND GLOBAL SEO

Now that we've discussed a bit about global keyword research, let's narrow our focus to the topic of geo-targeting and global SEO. This is where you tailor your website's content to appeal to audiences in various geographical locations. By taking advantage of geo-targeting, you can reach a wider range of potential customers and improve your standing in global search engine results.

Navigating the online world can be akin to journeying around the globe. There are different languages, cultures, and preferences to consider, and understanding these variations is key to tailoring your content effectively. Much like our world is divided into various countries and regions, the internet landscape can be seen as being segmented by different search engines and their respective regions of dominance.

Let's start with the basics. Geo-targeting is a tactic used to deliver different content to website visitors based on their geographic location. This can be as broad as a country or as specific as a city. Serving tailored content according to geographical location can enhance the user experience, making your content more relevant and accessible to your global audience.

For starters, it's crucial to know your audiences. Are they mostly based in one country or spread around the globe? This is important because search engines like Google use location data as one of their ranking factors. If your audience is primarily in Australia, for example, and your site is optimized for American English, your site might not rank as well in Australian search results.

Additionally, different cultures have different search habits. Just as you account for language in your optimization strategy, it's also crucial to factor in the cultural nuances of each region. Remember, SEO isn't just about reaching the most people; it's about reaching the right people. Engaging with your target demographic on a regional and cultural level can make all the difference in turning casual visitors into avid customers.

Understanding the legal and ethical factors of global SEO is equally important. While going global certainly opens up a wealth of new opportunities, it also comes with additional responsibilities. Privacy regulations, copyright laws, and data protection rules vary from country to country. Ensure your website is compliant with these regulations to avoid any potential issues.

Next, let's talk about the technology behind geo-targeting. IP detection is often used to determine a user's physical location. When a user visits your site, their IP address can be used to ascertain their general geographic area. You can then provide customized content based on this location. Keep in mind, though, that using IP addresses as a geographic indicator isn't foolproof. Proxy servers, VPNs, and mobile browsing can all impact the accuracy of this method.

In order to create a successful global SEO strategy, you need to ensure your URLs are unique for each targeted region. This helps search engines understand which version of your website to display to visitors based on their location. Using a site structure that includes subdomains or subdirectories with generic top-level domains (gTLDs) can achieve this. Alternatively, you might opt for using country-specific domains (ccTLDs).

Another critical aspect of global SEO is hreflang tags. These HTML attributes tell search engines which language you're using on a specific page of your website. This allows search engines to serve the most appropriate version of your site to users based on their language preference. By implementing hreflang tags correctly, you can dramatically improve your site's user experience and organic search visibility.

Sitemaps can also play a major role in your global SEO strategy. Not only do they help search engines understand your site's structure, but they also offer an excellent place to incorporate the hreflang tags mentioned earlier. Combine this with correct URL structure and you've got a recipe for global SEO success.

Finally, continually monitor your site's performance. As you start to implement these tactics, it's important to measure their effectiveness. Running regular audits and adjusting your strategies based on your findings will ensure that your SEO efforts are optimized for maximum impact across all geographic locations.

The world of geo-targeting and global SEO can seem a little daunting at first, but once you understand the basics and start implementing these strategies, you'll be well on your way to establishing a powerful global online presence. And remember, your worldwide domination begins with understanding and respecting the cultural, linguistic, and regional differences of your diverse audience.

Doing adequate research, implementing thoughtful strategies, and adapting based on data can be the difference between having a generic website and an engaging, geo-targeted site that truly resonates with your audience, regardless of where they're located on our globe. It's this thoughtfulness and care that can ultimately help your site go viral.

CHAPTER 6

Social Media: Your Global Viral Engine

Having scaled the heights of international SEO strategies in the previous chapters, it's time to dive into a reservoir of untapped potential - social media networks and their unrivaled ability to act as your global viral engine. There's no denying the prominence and power that social media wields in disseminating content far and wide, making it a critical tool for any website owner looking to create a viral sensation. From the eminent titans like Facebook, Twitter, and Instagram to rapidly emerging platforms such as TikTok and Snapchat, each offers unique opportunities to connect with diverse audiences, each with their distinct behaviors and preferences. But it's not just about getting your content out there; it's also about creating memorable, share-worthy content that resonates with your audience, sparking conversations, and fostering a sense of community. So, if you've been wondering how precisely to leverage social media channels and create content that spreads like wildfire, this chapter's got you covered!

LEVERAGING MAJOR SOCIAL NETWORKS

The beauty of living in our technologically advanced age is that you have access to platforms with user numbers that have reached and indeed veered into the billions. Facebook, Instagram, Twitter, LinkedIn, and others form this league of super-platforms. Each comes with a vast pool of potential customers ready for you to tap into. Let's dive into each one in depth, understanding the opportunities they offer to help your website go viral.

Facebook stands tall as the world's most popular and widely-used social network. With over 2.8 billion users, it warrants serious consideration in any campaign. Facebook offers various tools for businesses, including groups, pages, and advertisements, allowing you to tailor your content to your target audience in a way that can't just be ignored. Remember, the key here is to engage your audience with regular posts, prompt replies and incentivization through contests and giveaways.

Next arsenal in your chest comes Instagram. This visual-heavy platform has dominated the scene among younger audiences, making it ideal if this age group falls within your targeted customer base. It's a platform where aesthetic matters, so high-quality images and videos alongside a visually coherent theme can work wonders. You can also tag products in your posts, leading users directly to your site.

When it comes to immediacy and real-time engagement, nothing beats Twitter. It's a platform where news circulates, spurs conversations, and trends. Twitter thrives on hashtags, which can be used to tap into existing conversations or start a new one. Following trending topics and integrating them into your messaging can do wonders for your visibility on this platform.

For the professional crowd, LinkedIn has revamped itself from a job-seeking platform to a fulsome business and networking hub. Its members seek insightful articles, posts, and discussions regarding their industry. Creating and sharing thought leadership content here not only helps your website gain traction but also aids in positioning your brand as an industry leader.

But leveraging these major networks isn't just about uploading content and throwing out updates — it's about engagement and interaction. Many businesses make the mistake of treating social media as a megaphone, broadcasting messages without stopping to listen. The truth is, the most effective social media marketing is built on dialogue.

To stand out on these platforms, strive to spark conversations, drive discussions, and build relationships with your followers.

Besides, don't hesitate to utilize paid advertising programs that these platforms offer. While organic traffic is fabulous, paid ads can turbocharge your visibility, especially in the early stages of your company. Facebook Ads and Instagram sponsored posts, to name a few, offer in-depth targeting options allowing you to reach a razor-sharp focus on your ideal potential customer.

Moreover, the beauty of these platforms lies beyond their individual capabilities — they can work together, complementing each other and giving your brand a unified online presence. For instance, share your Instagram posts on your Facebook page to drive cross-traffic, or link to your latest blog post on both LinkedIn and Twitter.

One facet to keep note of is that each social network has its peak times. Posting at these times can make the difference in your post being seen by hundreds or thousands. Tools like HootSuite, Buffer, or Sprout Social can help determine these time slots and handle post scheduling for you, maximizing your reach at the best possible times.

Another instrumental feature present in these platforms is 'Analytics'. Every social platform provides robust analytic tools that present invaluable insights about your engagement rates, most popular posts, and much more, guiding you in crafting effective content strategies.

While each platform offers distinct features and audience characteristics, your brand's tone and personality should remain consistent throughout. This cohesiveness helps users recognize your brand and forms the basis for a strong brand identity that can bolster customer loyalty.

Moreover, remember that leveraging these platforms is not a one-time deal. The digital landscape is constantly evolving, with social networks hiking their game, rolling out new features, and modifying their algorithms regularly. It's necessary to stay alert and adapt your strategy according to these changes for maintaining your competitiveness.

In the grand scheme of things, patience is pivotal. Going viral rarely happens overnight. Continually promoting your site, engaging with your audience, and optimizing your strategy in light of analytics can light the slow-burning fuse that will eventually lead to your site's explosion onto the viral scene.

Finally, don't restrict yourself to these platforms. While these are certainly among the 'major leagues', other platforms and online communities are always worth exploring and experimenting with, especially those where your target audience tends to hang out.

To sum it up, thriving in the world of social media can seem labyrinthine, but remember that the center of it all are people - your potential customers. By focusing on them – their needs, interests, and habits – and then matching your strategy to meet them, you're well on your way to leveraging these networks for viral success.

EXPLORING EMERGING SOCIAL PLATFORMS

You've conquered the fundamentals of leveraging established social networks like Facebook, Twitter, and LinkedIn. Now, why not delve deeper and explore emerging social platforms? In the rapidly evolving digital landscape, up-and-coming social media platforms offer fresh opportunities for your website to go viral. With each new platform comes a unique audience with its own preferences, providing you with the chance to diversify and expand your reach.

Truth be told, navigating the ever-changing social media landscape can be quite a roller coaster ride. Today's hot social platform could be tomorrow's digital wasteland. However, what's key is that you stay ahead of the curve, and that means remaining in the know about the newest social media sites on the block.

Remember that success in viral marketing isn't always about being on every platform. Rather, it's about finding the platforms that resonate with your brand and audience. Whether it's a platform with a focus on short video content, like TikTok, or virtual hangout spaces like Clubhouse, your job is to identify where your target audience is hanging out and engage them effectively with shareable content.

Do your homework. Evaluate new social media platforms thoroughly before diving in. Consider things like the user demographics, popular content types, and the level of user engagement. These insights will help you to gauge whether a particular platform aligns with your brand and audience.

For instance, if you're catering to a younger demographic, platforms like Snapchat or TikTok can be goldmines of opportunity. These platforms support creative short-form content and thrive on a sense of spontaneity. Alternately, if your website relies heavily on visually appealing content, platforms like Instagram and Pinterest might be more up your alley.

It's also crucial to be familiar with the interface and features of each platform. For instance, Instagram has Stories, IGTV, and even Shopping features, while Twitter has recently added Fleets and Spaces. These features can significantly affect the type of content you create, how you interact with your audience, and the overall user experience, ultimately influencing the viral potential of your content.

Align your content strategy with each platform's unique mechanics and ethos. Static images may work great on Instagram, but videos might be the magic formula on TikTok. Similarly, fun, light-hearted content might get you noticed on Snapchat, while informative, thought-provoking pieces might resonate better on LinkedIn.

Don't disregard the power of influencers either. Emerging social networks often have a crop of early users who've built significant followings. Collaborating with these influencers can help your content reach a wider audience faster.

Set your KPIs before launching your viral campaign on any new platform. It's important to clarify what success looks like for your campaign, whether it's increased website traffic, higher brand engagement, or more product sales.

Remember to capitalize on specific trends unique to each platform. Trendjack if you must, but always respect the user community and form an authentic voice that meshes seamlessly with the prevailing culture.

However, it is important not to get lost or overwhelmed in the sea of these emerging trends. Monitor your performance regularly and adapt as needed. If a platform isn't bringing the desired results, or if another platform better aligns with your goals, don't hesitate to pivot.

Lastly, keep in mind that building a following on any social platform takes time and consistent effort. Don't get discouraged if your content doesn't go viral overnight. Keep producing, keep sharing, and keep engaging. An audience is more likely to share your content if they feel a genuine connection to your brand.

In this digitally charged era, the potential to ignite a global viral phenomenon is directly at your fingertips. Recognize that in the world of social media, innovation is fundamental, and change is the only constant. So be bold, be patient, and prepare for a thrilling adventure as you dive into exploring emerging social platforms. Remember, going viral isn't a sprint, but a marathon.

CREATING VIRAL SOCIAL MEDIA CONTENT

As we delve deeper into online content creation, your true tool for global virality rests in the art of producing engaging content specifically engineered for social media. What's the secret to breaking the internet? Frankly speaking, there's no cookie-cutter formula, but certain elements improve the likelihood of your content being shared far and wide. Once you master the essentials of creating viral social media content, you'll gain a formidable ally in your quest for digital dominance.

The first step is to understand that the content should be about the audience, not about you or your product. Creating shareable content often requires a shift in perspective. It's less about broadcasting your message, and more about creating something that will resonate with your audience on an emotional level. The substance that touches a chord is often the one that transcends into the infectious world of virality.

The nature of virality is unpredictable, and often, content does become an overnight sensation without any specific intent. However, a more reliable approach is to analyze viral trends and imbibe the lessons they offer. Reflecting on past viral phenomena offers insights into audience preferences, be they hilarious memes, moving stories, enlightening infographics, or awe-inspiring photos.

Digital storytelling is at the core of creating viral content. Tell your brand's story in a compelling, authentic way that captures the imagination of your audience. Good storytelling fosters engagement and motivates shares. It could be a video explainer about your brand's origins or an infographic how-to guide related to your niche. The primary goal is to demonstrate value and create a unique connection with your audience.

Humor is a universal language. If you can make your audience laugh, most of the work is done. Not only does it engage the audience, but it also encourages them to share the light-hearted mood with their friends. However, humor should be used mindfully. Nothing falls flatter than a joke that doesn't land or worse, offends your audience.

The role of visuals in creating viral social media content cannot be underestimated. A picture speaks a thousand words, and a well-placed GIF or meme could possibly express even more. Studies show that people are more likely to share visual content, like videos, infographics, and images, because they are immediately engaging and easily digestible.

Never underestimate the power of a good headline. You might have the most engaging and shareable content, but without a captivating headline, you run the risk of your content never being viewed. A good headline piques interest, promises value, and compels clicks. But remember, no clickbait. Once audiences realize they've been duped, they're unlikely to share the content or trust your brand in the future.

Controversy sparks discussion, and content that brings up different points of view tends to generate discussions on social media. This doesn't mean creating content that offends, rather meaningful, clear-eyed exploration of hot-button topics relevant to your brand and audience. But tread carefully, having a measured approach wards off potential backlash.

Incentivizing shares is also an effective way of stimulating viral social media content. Audiences are more inclined to distribute content when there's something in it for them. This could take the form of a promotional discount, the chance to win a competition, or even the simple satisfaction of seeing their name featured in a community post.

Let's not forget about the role of influencers in viral social media content. Collaborating with influencers who align with your brand image can drive engagement, expand your reach, and trigger shares. Influencers already have a loyal following that trusts their recommendations, tapping into this could boost your content's chances of going viral.

Creating a sense of urgency by making the content time-sensitive also encourages shares. Content based on trending topics, recent events, or limited-time promotions encourages the audience to share it right away.

Interactive content such as quizzes, contests, polls or surveys engages the audience and motivates them to share the fun with their friends. The role of gamification in producing viral hits cannot be understated. People enjoy being part of a game, challenge, or contest, and they often invite others to join in.

Focusing on positive content is an age-old trick proven by multiple studies. People are more likely to share content that is positive, inspiring, or heartwarming. There's enough negativity clouding digital media; let your content be the silver-lining.

Lastly, don't forget to include a strong call-to-action (CTA) to encourage social shares. Whether it's an invitation to share their thoughts, join a discussion, or share the content with friends, a well-placed CTA can make the difference between a widely-shared post and one that falls by the wayside.

Now that you know the vital ingredients for creating viral social media content, it's time to brew your unique concoction. Remember, while these strategies improve your chances, going viral isn't an exact science. What's key is to consistently create engaging content your audience appreciates and wants to share.

CHAPTER 7

Using Analytics for Global Success

If you're serious about making your website go viral globally, it's high time we talked about the importance of web analytics. They're not just a bunch of cold, hard facts and statistics. Instead, think of them as your secret weapon. After all, what's cooler than letting solid, reliable evidence guide your strategy to the top? Well, that's exactly what web analytics are for. Understand the basics first: Knowing what bounce rate, unique visitors, page views, or average session duration mean. With that bedrock of knowledge, you can then use analytics to gauge your website's virality. See which of your content is shared the most, which posts keep visitors hooked, and where in the world these visitors are coming from. Of course, the beauty of analytics doesn't stop there. This treasure trove of data doesn't just give you hard truths about your website, it also empowers you to make intelligent, data-driven decisions. With it, you can pinpoint what's working, ditch what's not, and continuously refine your strategy for global viral success. So, let's not underestimate the power of analytics - they're the compass that'll guide us on the path to global virality.

UNDERSTANDING WEB ANALYTICS BASICS

In the quest for global viral success, understanding the basics of web analytics is a must. Like a compass guiding a ship, web analytics can steer your website towards achieving your digital goals. Don't know where to start? Don't worry, that's what this section is designed for. By the end of this part, you'll feel confident using web analytics to your advantage.

What are Web Analytics? Well, in essence, web analytics is the measurement, collection, analysis, and reporting of web data to understand and improve web usage. In layman's terms, it's the process of translating your audience's online behavior into meaningful, actionable insights.

Imagine you're hosting a birthday party. What matters most? Sure, decorations, food, and music are all important. But the party's success ultimately depends on the guests. Are they interacting? Enjoying the food? Dancing to the music? Analyzing this data is key to throwing a successful party. The same idea applies to your website. Visitors are the guests, and analytics is your means to understand them better.

Who Uses Web Analytics? While once the domain of large corporations, web analytics are now used by business owners of all sizes, bloggers, nonprofits, governments, and marketers. If you have a website and you're interested in improving it, you're a potential user of web analytics.

Why Use Web Analytics? By analyzing web data, you can discover patterns, trends, and insights about your online visitors. Which pages do they like? Where do they come from? How long do they stick around? All of these questions are critically important to understand your audience and boost your website's performance. Web analytics provides the answers.

Key Terms in Web Analytics. As with any new subject, there's going to be a bit of jargon to sift through. Here are some of the key terms you'll want to familiarize yourself with:

Unique Visitors: The number of distinct individuals who visit your website during a given period.

Page Views: A count of the number of times a page has been viewed or loaded by your visitors.

Bounce Rate: The percentage of visitors who enter your site and then leave ("bounce") rather than continuing to view other pages within your site.

Conversion Rate: The percentage of visitors who take a desired action on your website. This might include making a purchase, subscribing to a newsletter, or sharing content.

Armed with an understanding of these terms, you can read and interpret web analytics reports, enhancing your confidence in managing your website.

Types of Web Analytics. There are three primary types of web analytics: Descriptive, Predictive, and Prescriptive. Descriptive analytics tells you what happened, such as how many visitors you had last month. Predictive analytics estimates what will happen in the future – for instance, predicting traffic peaks. Lastly, prescriptive analytics provides recommendations on how to act on the information, suggesting actionable steps to improve your website.

Web Analytics Tools. There's a whole heap of web analytics tools available to you. Google Analytics, Adobe Analytics, and Woopra are just a few examples. Each offers an array of features to help you gather and analyze data. So, picking the right one comes down to your specific needs, budget, and personal preference.

Interpreting Web Analytics. When gazing at web analytics, don't just look at the data - dive into it, decipher it, dissect it. By doing so, you'll uncover valuable insights. Why did your bounce rate suddenly increase? Is there a correlation between your website's loading speed and your conversion rate? Spot underlying trends and patterns, and you're on your way to making informed strategic decisions for your site's success.

Making Web Analytics Work for You. Web analytics isn't just about collecting data; it's about making the data work for you. If you realize your page views are overshadowed by a high bounce rate, maybe you're attracting the wrong traffic, or your website design needs a closer look. High conversion rates indicate you're doing something right, keep it up!

Common Challenges in Web Analytics. Deciphering web analytics isn't always a smooth ride. You might encounter data discrepancies due to various reasons like tracking errors, cookie deletions, and bot traffic. These challenges can distort your data, hence it's crucial to be aware of them and employ methods to overcome them.

Remember, just like chemistry or coding, mastering web analytics requires time and practice. But with patience, persistence, and a commitment to learning, you'll cultivate a skill-set that can propel your website's global viral success.

The following sections will delve deeper into using analytics to measure virality and making data-driven decisions. Consider this section as an introduction to the topic, setting the stage for much-needed skills in your global viral success journey.

USING ANALYTICS TO MEASURE VIRALITY

Stepping further into the realm of analytics, we find ourselves needing to measure one of the most elusive yet powerful phenomena in the digital world - virality. Knowing how to use analytics to discern the viral potential of your content and understand the driving force behind it is an essential part of achieving global popularity.

Let's start by understanding the kind of data we should be seeking. To measure virality, we need to pay special attention to metrics like the number of shares, comments, reactions, click-through rates, and conversions. These measurements help determine the reach and engagement of your content, offering the first signs of potential virality.

Shares are the gold standard of virality. After all, the more often your content is shared, the further it reaches. By monitoring the number of shares over time and comparing this data against other pieces of content, you can identify potential viral hits early.

But it's not enough just to track the number of shares. It's equally important to look at user reactions and engagement. This can involve monitoring the ratio of likes, comments, and other reactions to the number of shares. A high engagement rate is usually an indicator of strong emotional resonance, which is a key driver of virality.

Click-through rates (CTR) also play a crucial role in measuring virality. After all, people often share content without actually reading or watching it. A high CTR indicates that your content is not just shareable, but also interesting enough to compel users to find out more. This increases the chances of further shares, hence increasing the potential for virality.

Finally, let's talk about conversions. Irrespective of the number of shares or the reach of your content, if it doesn't drive conversions, it can't be deemed truly successful. Ultimately, the amount of viral content that leads to conversions can exemplifies the effectiveness of your viral campaign.

After identifying the metrics, the next step is selecting appropriate analytics tools. There are many reliable tools available in the market such as Google Analytics, BuzzSumo, CrowdTangle, etc. These platforms can help track your most viral content, shares, likes, comments, and backlinks, providing you with a comprehensive picture of your content's viral journey.

One common misconception about measuring virality is that you can only track it after the fact. However, a good analytics strategy should allow you to spot viral content as it's taking off. This gives you the opportunity to capitalize on a piece of content's viral potential, promoting it further or even creating spin-off content to keep the momentum going.

As you delve into your analytics, you'll likely notice certain patterns - times when your content tends to do particularly well, types of content that are more likely to go viral, or even the kinds of headlines that garner more shares. Don't ignore these patterns. Instead, leverage them to your advantage: create more of the content that does well, post it at the times when your audience is most active, and craft your headlines in a way that has proven successful in the past.

A word of caution, though. Remember that although analytics can give you insights into what tends to work, there are no guarantees in this game. Virality can sometimes stem from the most unexpected places. Therefore, keep experimenting and don't be afraid to take risks.

Keep in mind also that the global landscape adds another level of complexity. What goes viral in one region might not have the same impact elsewhere, due to cultural, linguistic, and societal differences. Be sure your analytics strategy accounts for these variations, and doesn't simply assume that what works in one market will automatically work in another.

In the end, remember that virality is not the sole measure of success. It's a piece of the puzzle, an by understanding it, you'll craft better campaigns for your global audience. It's part of a much larger tableau that includes solid content creation, smart SEO tactics, and an adaptable social media strategy.

Ultimately, the goal isn't becoming an overnight sensation with a one-hit wonder, but building an enduring global presence that consistently produces shareable, engaging content. By harnessing the power of analytics and understanding how to measure virality, you'll be well-prepared to reach this goal.

MAKING DATA-DRIVEN DECISIONS

Now that we've grasped the fundamentals of web analytics and how to use them to measure virality, let's delve into one of the most critical aspects of successful website management – making data-driven decisions. Understanding the data is one thing, but using it to guide your decisions is where the real power lies.

Decisions driven by genuine, insightful data allow you to sculpt your site and content to suit your audience better. It's not just about going with your gut, but balancing intuition with empirical evidence. You can fine-tune every aspect, from the content you create, the design of your site to your global SEO tactics.

Consider your website analytics as your navigation system. It's checking the current health of your platform, giving you insight into what's working, and more importantly, what isn't. The key here is taking that information and applying it to future strategies. You are not only reacting to the data but anticipating and planning for future shifts.

For instance, if your analytics reveal an uptick in traffic from a geographical location you didn't initially target, it's a clear indicator there's untapped potential. In this scenario, adapting your SEO strategy to appeal to this new audience could be advantageous.

Or let's say your data points out that a specific kind of content is averaging more shares and comments than others. That's your audience telling you what they like. Leaning into those preferences by producing more of the same type of content can potentially drive even more engagement and sharing.

Another aspect of making data-driven decisions involves using A/B testing. This kind of testing involves making a single change in a controlled variable (like the color of a call-to-action button or headline phrasing) while keeping everything else constant. Doing so allows you to determine which variable performs better. Integrating ongoing A/B testing into your processes can incrementally improve website performance and effectiveness over time.

Conversely, when the data shows that certain strategies aren't working, it's essential to pivot. Holding on to tactics just because they worked in the past is a pitfall that many websites succumb to. If the data consistently shows that something isn't working, don't hesitate to change your course.

Now, making data-driven decisions also means understanding some metrics matter more than others. Essentially, you need to identify your key performance indicators (KPIs), the metrics that matter most to your specific business and goals. Your KPIs may include things like pages per session, bounce rate, or conversion rate. Focusing on your KPIs helps you pay attention to the metrics that truly move the needle.

Moreover, remember that making data-driven decisions isn't about staring at spreadsheets all day. It's about spotting patterns, digesting what the numbers mean, and taking decisive action. In other words, data should inform decisions, not paralyze them.

We can't talk about making data-driven decisions without discussing the danger of becoming too obsessed with data. While it's crucial to listen to what the data tells you, remember that data is not infallible. Sometimes, the data can point you in the wrong direction, especially when it's incomplete or misinterpreted. Balancing data-driven decisions with a dose of human intuition and common sense is often the best approach.

Moreover, keep in mind that data, while valuable, is merely one piece of the puzzle. Understanding your audience isn't just about crunching numbers—it's also about empathy, human insight, and occasionally, taking calculated risks. Don't lose sight of the bigger picture.

Making data-driven decisions is, ultimately, a constant cycle of testing, learning, and optimizing. As you make these decisions, be patient with yourself and your website. It may take time, but the results you'll see from truly understanding your analytics and how to apply them will be well worth it. Your chosen path to virality should be dictated by the data, but guided by your intuition and your brand's unique presence and voice within the market.

In the end, the key to making smart, data-driven decisions is to keep learning. Virality isn't a precise science, and there will always be surprises. But by gathering as much data as possible and applying it in a measured, thoughtful way, you're setting yourself up for the best chance at global success.

CHAPTER 8

Case Studies: Successful Global Websites

After covering the essentials of building a global viral website, it's beneficial to gain insights from those who have already walked the path. This chapter explores captivating case studies of some of the most successful global websites. Each one offers valuable insights into achieving international virality.

CASE STUDY 1: DUOLINGO

Our first case study, **Duolingo**, is an example of a website that found the value of localization. Originally an English-only platform, Duolingo quickly realized the potential of multilingual provisions and capitalized on it. The decision to localize their website to accommodate multiple languages was pivotal in their global success. A combination of intuitive user interface, beautiful design, and intriguing gamification elements have made their website viral among language learners worldwide. Duolingo offers insight into the power of language personalization and thoughtful design.

CASE STUDY 2: AIRBNB

The success of **Airbnb** hinges on how its website design and functionality appeals to a global audience. Recognizing that accommodation is a universal necessity, Airbnb provides listings from all over the world with comprehensive descriptions, reviews, and ratings. User-generated content, coupled with a simple and intuitive user interface, enables Airbnb to maintain its steady growth.

Furthermore, their smart use of Search Engine Optimization (SEO) has helped users easily find their site when planning trips abroad. Their success story represents the importance of quality user-generated content and an emphasis on usability and SEO.

CASE STUDY 3: GREENPEACE INTERNATIONAL

Greenpeace International made waves with their global website that utilized social media to extend their reach and mobilize a broader community. With a strong call-to-action and an emotional allure, they could engage users and even catalyze them to participate. They adapted their messaging to resonate with different cultures and languages, reinforcing the power of localized content and social media integration.

CASE STUDY 4: ASOS

ASOS, a British online fashion and beauty retailer, went fully global by employing a comprehensive worldwide shipping strategy and localizing its website for various regions. With a detailed understanding of their global customers' unique requirements and tastes, ASOS personalized each user's experience. They highlight another way to achieve global reach: by identifying and addressing the specific wants and needs of different geographical markets.

CASE STUDY 5: AMAZON

Arguably the king of international websites, **Amazon** has meticulously built its cross-border business over two decades. Through solid delivery infrastructure, customer engagement, and comprehensive localization, Amazon has transformed from a simple online bookstore to a worldwide eCommerce mogul. It offers insights into the long-term strategic thinking required for global virality, demonstrating that it's more than just an impressive website—it's also about backend logistics and user-experience.

While these case studies provide insight into successful global website strategies, it's important to remember that there's no one-size-fits-all approach. Each business will have unique elements that contribute to its virality. As we look at these successful websites, we should focus on the principles they employ—understanding the global audience, localizing content, optimizing for SEO, leveraging social media, prioritizing user-experience, and making data-driven decisions—to help shape our own strategies.

Keep in mind that virality doesn't happen overnight. It requires painstaking effort, strategic planning, execution, and a lot of patience. The road may be challenging, but with each obstacle overcome, we get closer to attaining our goal. There are countless web success stories out there, and the exciting part is that the next one could be yours. But remember, the journey to global virality isn't just about trying to replicate the success of these companies—it's about understanding the nuances of your own business, defining what virality means to you, and applying the most relevant strategies effectively.

As we conclude this chapter, the goal is not to leave with a blueprint of what these giants did, but with an understanding of the principles that led to their success. Those same principles, appropriately applied, have the potential to drive your own company towards global virality. The case studies we've outlined here are a source of inspiration, a touchstone that allows you to measure your ideas and shed light on possibilities.

CONCLUSION

Your Global Viral Roadmap

In wrapping up, every website owner has the potential to create a global viral sensation—you've just got to find the mix that resonates. From understanding virality and nurturing organic growth, to effectively leveraging social media platforms and the power of SEO, we've blazed a trail that can lead to astounding viral success. But remember, in the ever-shifting digital landscape, staying alert to changing trends and agile in your approach will always be intrinsic to sustained viral growth. The journey doesn't end here; in fact, it's merely begun. Utilize your newfound insights from global website case studies, web analytics, and international SEO tactics to make data-driven decisions. Cultivate shares and lay the groundwork for your content to echo around the globe. Now, fully armed, it's your time to make your website the next viral star of the internet world.

TOP TIPS FOR VIRAL SUCCESS

Create Personable Content
People are drawn to content that is relatable and personal. Authentic storytelling can be a powerful tool to captivate your audience, engage them emotionally, and encourage them to share your content. Anecdotes, personal experiences, and user-generated content do wonders for building connections and driving shares.

Emotions are Key

In creating viral content, emotional resonance can't be overlooked. Content which sparks joy, surprise, humor, or even anger and sadness, has a higher chance of being shared. Make your audience feel something intensely, and they'll spread the word.

Keep it Simple and Catchy

Don't make your audience work too hard to grasp your message. Your content should be straightforward and catchy. The more easily digestible it is, the higher the chances for it to go viral. Simplistic content can spread like wildfire, capturing the attention of a vast audience.

Optimize for Shareability

Ensure that your content is super easy to share. Use social sharing buttons, call-to-actions, and mobile-friendly designs. Accessibility and ease of sharing dramatically affect the virality of your content.

Leaning on Trends and Pop Culture

Tap into the pulse of pop culture and trends. Incorporate trending topics, memes, and viral challenges into your content. It won't just make your content current and relatable, but also increase your content's probability of going viral. Just be sure to add your unique spin to it!

Timing Matters

The time you post your content plays a significant role. Understand the behavior and time zones of your audience. Make sure that you're publishing when they're most active. Timing can be a crucial factor for your content's viral potential. Research and schedule strategically!

Celebrate Participation and Engagement

People love being part of something big. Therefore, celebrate and appreciate audience engagement. Highlight top commenters, share user-generated content, and run contests. This will encourage them to engage further and share your content with their networks.

Inject Humor

Humor breaks barriers and makes content relatable. Virality and humor often go hand in hand. Strive to incorporate a funny twist or a comic relief moment in your content to engage your audience and make them hit that share button.

Values and Social Causes

Standing for a social cause gives purpose to your content. People tend to share content which resonates with their values or supports a cause they believe in. It gives them a sense of contributing positively by sharing your content.

Surprise and Delight

Create content that surprises and delights your audience. Unexpected turns, striking visuals, or exciting giveaways can make your content memorable. A delighted audience is more likely to share and spread the word.

Collaborations

Partner with influencers or other businesses that share your target audience. This not only expands your reach but adds credibility to your content. Collaborative content can often gain significant traction and go viral.

Empower Your Audience

Enabling your audience to shape your content gives them ownership and a reason to share. Invite them to vote, submit ideas or take part in developing your content. When your audience invests their time, they'll be willing to share the resulting content.

Continuously Test and Optimize

Aim for continuous improvement. Keep experimenting with different approaches, style, and formats until you find what resonates best with your audience. Use analytics to measure performance and optimize accordingly. What works for one may not work for the others, so be patient.

Quality Over Quantity

Spamming your audience with loads of content doesn't work. Focus on creating fewer pieces of top-notch, high-value content that'll impress your audience and encourage them to share. High-quality content speaks volumes and is more likely to go viral.

Stay Consistent

Consistency is key in maintaining your brand's voice and audience engagement. With consistent high-quality content, you can build an audience that trusts your brand and eagerly anticipates and shares your content. Consistency can be your biggest ally in creating viral content.

RECAP AND NEXT STEPS

Looking back on what's been covered in prior chapters, we've explored an expansive roadmap for setting your website up to capture the magic of viral content for a global audience. This isn't an overnight journey, but rather, a long-term investment that, with time and the right effort, can yield great success.

The initial foundational steps involve recognizing the power of virality and the underlying mechanics that can fuel it. This involves a deep understanding of your audience behavior and their sharing habits, which drive key factors in viral content creation.

With the distinction between organic and paid growth discussed, we emphasized the vitality of fostering organic growth. Practicing patience here is paramount. Natural, non-forceful methods often establish a sturdy base over time. However, it is also worth noting the power of paid growth strategies when executed appropriately.

In the journey to establish a global presence, we also touched on the importance of localizing your content to achieve global appeal. This is a step that can't be overlooked. Paying due consideration to language, culture, laws, and ethics is a must. It's about earning your audience's trust and creating a website that caters to their needs, values, and comfort.

In the realm of International SEO, we emphasized the essential role that global keyword research plays and the value of geo-targeting. These efforts work in tandem to make your website easily discoverable and relatable to a global audience.

By exploring how social media can act as your global viral engine, we've dived into the potential of major social networks and emerging platforms. Each has unique algorithms and populations that, if harnessed effectively, can dramatically amplify content reach and engagement.

Web analytics underpins many of the strategies laid out in previous chapters. It's a critical tool for understanding traffic flow, audience behavior, and engagement patterns. Even more, it can empower you to make data-driven decisions that consistently improve your website's appeal and performance.

Learning from successful global websites is one of the most effective ways to spur ideas for your own viral strategy. Rationalizing the strategies of successful viral websites and figuring out how to make those strategies work in your specific situation is an invaluable pursuit.

Having said all this, it's clear that going viral isn't a matter of luck. It requires diligent planning, analysis, and adaptation. Remember, virality is a constant journey of learning and tweaking, peppered with consistent action.

In respect to initiating your journey to global virality, the first step is to thoroughly digest the strategies discussed. Take ample time to digest the implications of these strategies on your current website context. This would involve analysing your existing content, understanding your current audience, and estimating the potential for virality.

Once this has been well pondered, sketch out a concrete plan. Detail your strategy considering your audience and the type of content that would resonate with them. Break this down further into the platforms you'll leverage, the localization techniques you'll apply, and how you'll differentiate organically from paid promotions.

Next, arm yourself with the right tools. This includes effective social media tools, SEO and Analytics tools. You should also maintain a detailed and active glossary, to keep you updated with the latest trends. Always stay in the loop, your attention and agility is what will set you apart.

It's time to put these plans into action. Start creating content, measure the engagement using analytics, fine-tune your strategies based on the data, and repeat. It's a constant cycle of creation, evaluation, and adaptation.

Now that we've revisited the roadmap, it's time to walk it. Go ahead, be persistent, be creative, and make your website go viral on a global scale.

APPENDIX A

Useful Tools for Viral Success

In your quest to achieve global viral success, certain tools can significantly streamline your efforts and optimize outcomes. First off, consider integrating a roster of social media tools—such as Buffer, Hootsuite, and CoSchedule—which allow for efficient scheduling and management across various platforms, thereby maximizing your reach. For search engine optimization, options such as SEMrush and Ahrefs offer a wealth of capabilities—from keyword research to competitor analysis—that can enhance your visibility. Finally, don't overlook the indispensable value of analytics tools. Google Analytics, for instance, provides a deep dive into your website's traffic trends and audience behavior, which in turn caters to data-driven decision making. Additionally, platforms like BuzzSumo can offer useful insights into what content is trending and resonating most with audiences in your domain. Remember, each tool serves a unique purpose, so make sure you're making the most of them in your strategy to go viral.

SOCIAL MEDIA TOOLS

When it comes to constructing a global, viral website, pairing up with the suitable social media tools is pivotal. They can help optimize and automate processes, manage various social media platforms, and analyze performance more efficiently. Let's delve into some of the most favorable social media tools to enhance your global viral success.

1. Buffer:

With Buffer, you can schedule posts across multiple platforms like Facebook, Twitter, LinkedIn, and Instagram. It offers time-saving tools for managing your social media marketing so that you can stick to creating engaging, viral content. The analytics feature helps you track customer engagement and understand the kind of content that works for your audience.

2. BuzzSumo:

This is a useful research tool that allows you to identify what content is popular by topic or on any website, hence what goes viral. With BuzzSumo, you can find key influencers in your niche and see what's being shared on social media platforms.

3. Hootsuite:

Hootsuite is a comprehensive social media management tool that allows you to schedule posts ahead of time, monitor the effectiveness of your content, and manage all your social media accounts from a single dashboard. It also comes with a range of analytics tools, allowing you to measure the success of your viral campaigns.

4. Sprout Social:

This tool offers a platform that marries deep analytics and effective social engagement. It's great for content planning and publishing, analytics, and engagement. With comprehensive reporting, you get a full understanding of how your content performs across platforms. And by using its CRM features, you can nurture relationships with audiences and influencers.

5. Canva:

Visual content plays a pivotal role in successful virality. With Canva, you can create eye-catching images and designs for your website and social media platforms without needing design expertise. Its drag-and-drop interface and extensive library of templates make it a user-friendly tool for creating professional-grade visuals.

The tools outlined above aren't an exhaustive list, but they're a good start for anyone trying to make their website go viral. When you align these tools with a sound social media strategy, you set up a strong foundation upon which virality can thrive.

Remember, these tools are helpful support systems, but they can't replace engaging, shareable content or healthy interactions with your audience. Make sure you're still focusing on those key areas as you explore these tools and how they can boost your global website's viral potential.

SEO TOOLS

Strengthening your website's search engine optimization (SEO) can be a game-changer in your endeavor to viral success. Fortunately, there are a multitude of SEO tools out there that can assist you in identifying gaps, formulating strategies, and measuring results. Let's dive into some of them.

Google Keyword Planner: The first tool that should be in your SEO arsenal is Google's Keyword Planner. It's incredibly powerful for finding the right keywords for your content, gauging their competitiveness, and identifying search volume trends. Remember, a great deal of your traffic will come from organic search, so targeting the right keywords is imperative for viral success.

SEMrush: If you're serious about SEO, SEMrush is worth considering. This comprehensive tool helps in keyword research, tracking keyword ranking, checks backlinks, scrutinizes competitor's SEO, and does a heck of a lot more. It's like a Swiss Army knife for all your SEO needs.

Moz: Another comprehensive SEO tool, Moz, offers resources to help you with all your SEO needs. It allows you to perform site audits, keyword research, and to track your website's rank for specific keywords. Plus, Moz's SEO toolbar plugin gives you instant metrics while viewing any webpage or SERP (search engine results page).

Ahrefs: Known for its backlink analysis, Ahrefs offers a comprehensive suite of SEO tools. It can help you with competitor analysis, keyword research, backlink research, content research, and rank tracking. It's a robust platform that can help you dig deep into your SEO metrics.

Screaming Frog SEO Spider: This efficient tool is particularly useful for conducting quick site audits. It can analyze your website proactively for broken links, analyze metadata and titles, generate XML sitemaps, discover duplicate content, and more. It's a workhorse for technical SEO.

Yoast SEO: If your website is on WordPress, Yoast SEO is a must-have plugin. It assists with creating search engine friendly content by analyzing your posts' readability, keyword usage, and more. It's a handy tool for both SEO beginners and savvy webmasters.

Value-wise, these tools are worth their weight in gold. Each tool offers unique features and benefits that, when used correctly, can aid significantly in your push for viral success. However, keep in mind that SEO tools are simply that - tools. They can give you the data and insight you need to make smart decisions, but the strategies and implementation must come from you.

In the next section, let's talk about equally vital tools, particularly those that help us understand the results of our efforts better -- Analytics tools.

ANALYTICS TOOLS

Alright, so, we've talked a lot about the importance of understanding your audience and data. At this point, you might be asking yourself how you're actually going to do that. How do you extract valuable insights from that daunting sea of data? Well, lucky for us, there are numerous analytics tools out there to help us on our journey to viral success. Let's dive deep into this toolbox and see what we can find.

Google Analytics

No discussion on web analytics can start without mentioning Google Analytics. It's the Godzilla of analytics tools, able to reveal who's visiting your site, what they're doing, and, more importantly, what's working and what's not. But perhaps its greatest value lies in its ability to track the origin of your web traffic and provide demographic information. The insights from Google Analytics can guide your efforts to optimize your site and content.

Kissmetrics

Ever wished you could follow your users around like a fly on the wall, observing every click and interaction? That's what Kissmetrics allows you to do. Dubbed as a 'person-based' analytics tool, Kissmetrics focuses on tracking the behavior of individual users. By providing insights into user behavior, it can help you understand what keeps people hooked on your site and that's pretty useful for viral ambition.

Crazy Egg

Imagine being able to see exactly where your visitors are clicking on your webpage. Crazy Egg offers heatmaps and scroll maps that give you a visual insight into your user behavior, showing you what's hot and what's not. It's like having X-ray vision for your website, and that can be incredibly valuable when you're striving for that viral hit.

BuzzSumo

Ah, BuzzSumo. This tool is like a goldmine for content marketers. BuzzSumo helps you identify the most shared content and trending influencers in your niche, giving you valuable insights into what goes viral in your industry. Armed with this info, you can design your content strategy to align with what your audience loves.

Summing it up...

Analytics tools are not just number-crunchers; they're your guide, mentor, and catalyst for viral success. They can provide you with the insights you need to understand what works, what doesn't, and what it takes for your content to hit the viral jackpot. So don't overlook the power of analytics tools. Make them an integral part of your website strategy, because understanding your audience is the key to viral success.

Up next, we'll deep dive into the Glossary, where we'll make sense of all these terms you've been learning. Stay tuned!

GLOSSARY

In the world of digital marketing and website management, we often come across some confusing jargon. These terms can sometimes be overwhelming, especially when you're trying to analyze your website's performance or planning your next big viral campaign. But, don't worry. We've got your back! This glossary defines some of the crucial, basic terms you will navigate through your journey towards virality.

A/B TESTING

This refers to the method of comparing two different versions of a webpage, ad, or piece of content to determine which one performs better.

ANALYTICS

A collection of data about a website or app's users and their behavior. This could include information about where users come from, how much time they spend on your site, and what actions they take.

CLICK-THROUGH RATE (CTR)

The percentage of your audience that advances (or clicks through) from one part of your website to the next step of your marketing campaign. Higher CTRs indicate more effective marketing material.

CONVERSION

The action of a user completing a desirable action on your website, such as filling out a form, purchasing a product, or becoming a member.

GEO-TARGETING

The practice of delivering targeted content or ads to consumers based on their geographical location.

ORGANIC GROWTH

The process of businesses expanding naturally rather than through paid advertising or marketing campaigns.

SEARCH ENGINE OPTIMIZATION (SEO)

A methodology of strategies, techniques, and tactics used to increase the number of visitors to a website by obtaining a high-ranking placement in search results of a search engine.

SOCIAL MEDIA ENGAGEMENT

Any form of interaction that users have with your social content (likes, comments, shares, retweets, etc.). It is a measure of the impact your content is making.

USER BEHAVIOR

The understanding of what users do while they are on your website - the actions they take, the content they interact with, the path they take through your site, etc.

VIRALITY

The phenomenon of a piece of content rapidly circulating or shared massively on the internet within a short period.

This glossary provides a base understanding of the terminology we've discussed so far, and it's a handy reference for you to return to, ensuring you're knowledgeable and well-armed for your journey to virality. Remember, words are the building blocks of communication. Master these, and you're well on your way to mastering the art of website virality.

www.ingramcontent.com/pod-product-compliance
Lightning Source LLC
Chambersburg PA
CBHW051212050326
40689CB00008B/1280